ᖃᓄᖅ ᐊᑎᖃᖅᐱᑦ?
What Is Your Name?

ᐅᖃᓕᒫᒐᖅ ᐃᓄᐃᑦ ᐊᑦᑏᔅᔪᓯᖕᒋᓐᓂᒃ
A Book about Inuit Naming Practices

ᑎᑎᖅᑐᖅ

ᑯᑭᒃ ᑯᓯᒐᖅ, ᓯᐊᕐ ᓇᐅᓪᓚᖅ ᐱᐊᓐᔨᒥᓐ ᐋᕆᐊᒃ, ᐸᓂᒍᓯᖅ ᐆᐱᑦ, ᐊᒻᒪ ᑖᒪᓂᒃ ᑎᒋᐊᐸᒃ ᐹᒡᓯᒪ

ᑎᑎᖅᑐᓚᖅᑐᖅ

ᐊᒦᐅᓪ ᓵᓐᑦᓚᓐᑦ

WRITTEN BY

Kukik Kusugak, Seth Naullaq Benjamin Arreak, Panigusiq Obed, and Dominic Tegeapak Bergsma

ILLUSTRATED BY

Amiel Sandland

ᐃᓄᖕᓄᑦ ᐊᑦᙯᓂᖅ ᐱᒻᒪᕆᐊᓗᖓᖅ.

ᓄᑕᕋᖅ ᐃᓅᒻᒪᑦ, ᐊᑦᓂᖅᑕᐅᔭᕐᓲᖑᖅ. ᐃᓄᐃᑦ ᓲᔪᔾᑦ ᐊᑦᓂᖅᑕᐅᓴᕐᒪᑕ ᐃᓚᒋᓕᐅᖅᑕᕐᓂᖓᓂᒃ ᐃᓅᔪᓂᖅᓯᒪᔪᓂᒃ. ᑕᐃᒪᒃ ᓴᖅᑭᑎᑎᖅ ᐃᓚᒥᔪᐸ ᐱᒻᒪᐅᓂᓂᒃ. ᑕᐃᒪᐃᑎᒻᒍ ᐃᑲᔪᑎᖅᔪᖅ ᐃᓚᔭᓂᑦ ᐃᖅᑲᐅᒪᑎᑎᕙᒻᒪᑕ ᖃᓂᖕᓯᐊᓇᖅᑑᑎᓪᓗ ᓇᐅᒻᒍᖅᓯᒪᕝᕙᒻᒪᕐᒪ.

Naming is important to Inuit.

When a child is born, they are given a name. Inuit children are usually named after a family member who has died. This shows that the family member is important. It helps a family remember and stay connected to someone who is gone.

ᐃᓱᒪᒋᓚᐅᖅᓯᒪᕕᐅᒃ ᐊᑏᑦ? ᐊᑦᑎᖅᑕᐅᓯᒪᕕᑦ ᐃᓚᔫᓐᓄᑦ ᐱᓐᓇᕆᔭᐅᔪᒥᒃ?

ᐃᓄᐃᑦ ᓱᕈᑦᑎᑦ ᐅᓂᒃᑳᒃᓴᖅᑲᐅᒻᒪᕆᓲᖑᔪᑦ ᐊᑎᖏᑕ ᒥᒃᓵᓄᑦ. ᐅᓂᒃᑳᑦ ᐅᑯᐊ ᓱᕈᓰᑦ ᑎᓴᒪᑦ ᐊᑎᖏᓐᓂᒃ.

Have you ever thought about your name? Were you named after someone special to your family?

Inuit children have important stories to tell about their names. Here are the stories of four children's names.

ᐊᑎᕋ ᑯᑭᒃ.

My name is Kukik.

4

ᐅᓇ ᐊᑖᑕᒪ.

This is my father.

ᐅᓇ ᐊᑖᒐ ᐊᖁᓂᕐᔭᕐᒃᓇ. ᐊᑎᑎᑕᐅᖅᑕᖕᓇ ᑯᑭᒃ ᑯᓱᒐᖅ.

ᐊᑎᖅᖅᑐᖕᓇ ᐊᑖᒐ ᐊᖁᓂᕐᔭᐃᓂᖕᓂᒃ. ᐊᒪᐅᑎᑕᐅᖅᔪᒪᕝᕝ.

ᐊᑎᕐ ᑯᑭᒃ.

ᐊᒪᐅᑎᑕᐅᖅᑕᕐᕝ ᐃᓕᖕᕐᑎᕐᓄᒃ ᓯᕐᑕᕐᑎᑕᐅᖅᑐᖅ. ᒥᖅᓱᖅᑰᔪᖕᓂᓂ. ᓯᑐᖅᕓᐊᔪᖕᓂᓂ ᐃᖕᖃᓂᖅᑐᓂᔪ. ᐃᕐᖓᑕᕐᕐᓂᖕᓂᒃ ᐱᓕᕆᐅᔭᓕᖅᑎᑎᖅᕌᑕᑕᐅᖅᑐᖅ.

This is my father's grandmother. Her name was Kukik Kusugak.

I am named after my father's grandmother. She was my great-grandmother.

My great-grandmother was our family's leader. She was very good at sewing. She was smart and kind. She made her grandchildren feel special.

ᐊᒪᐅᓈᓐᒃ ᐊᑎᖃᕐᓂᕐᐱᑦ, ᐃᓚᔾᔭᓄᑦ ᑐᖅᓯᕐᖄᑕᐅᑎᐊᖅᐸᒃᑐᖕᓂ, ᑐᖅᓯᕐᖄᐸᒃᑲᕋᑦ ᑐᒻᑦᓪᓗ! ᑐᖅᓯᕋᕐᓂᕐᒦ ᑕᐃᔭᐅᔦᕐᖅ.

ᐊᑖᑦᓯᕐᐊᕋᒪ ᑕᐃᕓᖃᖕᓂ "ᐊᓈᓇᓪᖅ" ᐊᑎᖃᓂᕐᓄᑦ ᐊᓈᓇᖕᓂᓂᒃ. "ᐊᓈᓇᓪᖅ" ᑐᖅᑎᒃ "ᐊᓈᓇᖅᓪᕐᒃ."

ᐅᐱᒡᑎᐊᖅᑐᖕᓂ ᐊᑎᖃᕋᒪ ᑯᕐᒦᒃ ᐊᑎᑎᐊᖕᔪᖕᓪᑦ ᐱᒡᓕᓇᐅᑦᑐᓂᑦ ᐃᓚᔾᔭᓄᑦ.

Because I am named after my great-grandmother, people in my family have special names for me, and I have special names for them! These are called "kinship terms."

My grandfather calls me "Anaanalaaq" because I am named after his mother. "Anaanalaaq" means "little mother."

I am proud to be named Kukik because it is a beautiful name that is special to my family.

ᐊᑎᖅᖅᑐᖕᒐ ᓇᐅᓪᓚᕐᒥᒃ.

My name is Naullaq.

ᐅᓇ ᐊᓈᓇᒪ.

This is my mom.

11

ᐅᓇ ᐊᖕᒪᒪ. ᐊᓈᓇᒪ ᐊᓂᒍᓗᖕᖁᓂᒃ ᐊᖕᔨᑉᑎᖃᖅᐸᖅ.

ᐊᑎᖅᖁᑐᖕᒐ ᐊᖕᒫᓂᒃ. ᐊᑎᖅᖁᓯᒪᖕᒦᕋᖅ ᐊᔭᐅᐸᐱᐊᖕᓂᒃ. ᓇᐅᓪᓚᖅ ᐃᓚᔭᕈᑎᖕᓄᑦ ᐱᓪᒪᑎᐊᔪᔭᒥᕗ.

This is my uncle. He is my mom's oldest brother.

I am named after my uncle. He was named after my great-great-grandfather. Naullaq is a very important name in our family.

13

ᐃᓅᕋᑦᖅᑎᓐᓂᑐᖕᓂ, ᓂᖕᒥᑎᒡᒪ ᓂᕕᐊᖅᓯᐊᒃ ᑕᑯᖅᑐᓚᐅᖅᓯᒪᓕᖕᓂ.
ᐅᖄᓚᐅᖕᐱᕐᑕᐅᖅᓯᒪᓕᖕᓂ ᐃᖕᒋᒥᑐᒃ ᓇᐅᓪᓚᖅᑐᒃ, ᐊᖕᓪᓚ,
ᑐᖅᑯᕐᐱᓂᖅ ᐃᓅᑕᐅᖅᑎᖁᓇᖕᓂ. ᐅᖅᑲᑕᐅᖅᓯᒪᓕᕙᖅ ᐊᑯᓂᐊᓗᒡᖅ
ᐊᐅᖕᓚᖅᓯᓚᑕᐅᖅᑐᖕᓂ ᐅᑎᑕᐃᖅᑱᖅᑐᖕᓂ. ᓂᖕᒋᑕᑦ ᐅᖅᑱᖅᓯᓚᕐᖅ
ᖅᑯᖕᓚᓚᐃᒪᓚᒡᖅ, ᖅᑯᐊᐊᕐᖕᓯᒡᑐᖕ ᖅᐱᐊᔾᖅ.

ᓯᖅᑲᐃᕝᒪ ᐊᑎᖅᑲᒡᒪ ᐊᔾᓚᖕᓄᖅ, ᐃᓚᖁᒐᓄᖅ ᑕᐃᒍᕐᖅᖄᐅᐱᕐᕋᖕᓄᖅ
ᑐᖅᕐᖅᐅᑎᖕᓂᖅ, ᑐᖅᕐᖅᒥᕐᖅᖄᖕᖅᑕᐅᖅᖅᑕᐅᖅᑐᖅ!

ᓂᖕᒋᑎᒡᒪ ᓂᕕᐊᖅᓯᐊᒃ ᑐᖅᕐᖅᖅᖅᐸᒃᖅᖕᓂ "ᐃᕐᓂᖅ" ᐊᑎᖅᑯᓯᓅᖕᓂᖅ
ᐃᕐᓂᖕᒥᓂᖅ.

ᑐᖅᕐᖅᖅᑕᕐ "ᐊᓈᓇ."

When I was a newborn baby, my grandmother Niviaqsiaq came to see me. She spoke to me like I was her son Naullaq, my uncle, who died before I was born. She said that I had been away for a long time and had finally come back. My grandmother says that I smiled, and that made her cry tears of happiness.

Because I am named after my uncle, people in my family have special kinship terms for me, and I have special kinship terms for them!

My grandmother Niviaqsiaq calls me "Irniq" because I am named after her son. "Irniq" means "son."

I call her "Anaana," which means "mother."

ᐊᑎᕐ ᐱᕐᖃᓂᔭᕐᑕ, ᓇᐅᓪᓚᖅ, ᐊᑎᕐ ᐱᕐᖃᓂᔭᐅᒡᒪᑦ ᐃᓚᑦᖃᐅᑎ ᐊᒥᓱᓂᖅ ᐱᕐᖁᑎᖃᖅᑑᑎᖅ.

I like my name, Naullaq, because the name is special to my family for many reasons.

ᐊᑎᕐ ᐸᓂᒍᓯᖅ.

My name is Panigusiq.

ᐅᐊ ᐊᐁᐅᒪ.

This is my mom.

ᐅᓇ ᓂᐳᑎᐅᕘ. ᐊᓈᓇᒪ ᐊᓈᓇᖕᓗ. ᐊᑎᖅᑕᐅᖅᑐᖅ ᒥᐊᓕ
ᐸᓂᒍᓯᖅ ᑲᓴᕐᒥᑦ.

ᐊᑎᖅᖅᑐᕐᓚ ᓂᐳᑎᐅᓄᖅ. ᐊᑎᕋ ᑐᑭᖅᖅᑐᖅ
"ᐸᓂᒐᖖᒥᑦ."

ᐊᒥᓲᑦ ᑕᐃᓯᕐᖁᓇᑎᖅᖅᐸᖕᒥᑦᑐᑦ ᐊᑎᓐᓂᖅ. ᐃᓚᖕᒥᓄᑦ
ᑕᐃᔅᐅᑐᐃᖕᓇᖅᖃᑦᑐᕐᓕ "ᐸᓐ"-ᒥᑦ. ᐃᑲᕐᔭᖅᐸᒃᑕᒃᑭ
ᐊᑎᓐᓂᑦ ᑕᐃᓯᑎᐊᖅᑎᓐᓇᕐᔪᑐᕋᑦ, ᐸᓂᒍᓯᕐᒥᑦ. ᐊᑎᕋ
ᐅᐱᒋᔭᒐ.

This is my grandmother. She is my mom's mom. Her name was
Mary Panigusiq Cousins.

I am named after my grandmother. My name means "darling
daughter."

Most people have a hard time saying my name. Some people
just call me "Pun." But I always try to help them say my full
name, Panigusiq. I am very proud of my name.

ᓂᕐᐴᓂ ᐊᑎᖅᓯᓄᓪᒍᑦ, ᑐᖅᓱᕐᖅᑕᐅᖁᑐᖁᖅ ᐱᓐᓇᑎᝪᐊᑦᓄᖁ.

ᐊᖅᓇᒪ ᐃᑦᒪᓄᒃᑐᑦ ᑐᖅᓱᕐᖅᐸᑦᒃᖁ "ᐊᖅᓇ"-ᒥᓄᖅ ᐊᖅᓇᖁᓂᖅ ᐊᑎᕐᖅᖅᒪ.

ᐊᖅᓇᒪ ᐱᖅᖄᓐᕐᖁᑦᖁ ᐃᓯᖁᓄᑦ ᑕᐃᕐᐸᑅᒪᒥᕐᕐᖁ "ᒥᕐᔅ ᓰ." ᑕᐃᒪᖁ ᓂᕐᐸᑅ ᐃᓯᐃᐱᕐᐅᓇᑐᖅᒑᒪᓐᒪᑦ ᐊᑎᕐᕐᖁᕐᐅᑐᖅᒑᒪᖁᒪᑦ ᖃᕐᖁᒥᖅ.

Because I am named after my grandmother, some people have special kinship names for me.

My mother sometimes calls me "Anaana" because I am named after her mother.

One of my mother's friends calls me "Mrs. C." That is because my grandmother was a teacher and her last name was Cousins.

ᐅᐱᒪᑦᑎᐊᖅᑑᖕᓇ ᓂᕐᔪᑏᖕ ᐊᑏᓕᓐᑯᖅ. ᑲᑎᒪᐅᖅᓲᒐᖕᒥᑦᑕᖅ,
ᑭᓴᐊᓂ ᐅᓂᒃᑲᓕᕐᒪᖕᑕᖅ. ᐊᖃᓇᐅ ᐅᖅᖅᐸᑐᖅ ᓂᕐᔪᖕᓂ
ᐊᕐᖳᖅᓂᓐᓂᒃ. ᖅᑯᐊᐊᕐᔭᖕ ᑕᑐᕐᓇᖅᑐᑎᓕᐅᑎᐊᖕᓐᖅ,
ᑕᐅᔭᑐᓇᖅ. ᐊᖃᓇᐅ ᐅᖅᖅᐸᑐᖅ ᐊᖃᓐᓗᑯᔾᖅ
ᖅᓂᓐᓘᑎᐸᐸᑲᖅ.

I am proud that I am named after my grandmother. I never met her, but I like to talk about her. My mom says I am a lot like my grandmother. I love art and so did she. My mom says I make her feel very close to her mother.

ᐊᏂᓯ Ċᒪᓂᖕ Ꮒᒥᐊᐸᖕ.

My name is Dominic Tegeapak.

ᐃᓇ ᓂᖕᒥᐳᕐ ᓄᐊᕐ. ᐊᓈᓇᒪ ᐊᓈᓇᖕ.

This is Nana Nora. She is my mother's mother.

ᐅᓇ ᐊᒪᐅᖅ. ᓂᕐᒋᐅᖅᒪᕐ ᓄᐊᖅᐅᐸ ᐊᐦᑖᖕᓇ. ᐊᑎᖅᑲᐅᖅᑐᖅ ᔫᒥᓯ ᑎᕐᐊᐸᖕᒦᖅ.
ᓂᕐᒋᐅᖅᒪ ᓄᐊᖅᐅᐸ ᐊᑎᖅᓯᓕᓐᕐ ᐊᒪᐅᖕᓂᖅ.

ᐅᖅᐅᕐᐠᐅᐦᑐᖕᓂ ᐊᒪᐅᓔᑎᐊᖅᑐᖕᓐᔫᖅ. ᑕᒥᓇᖅᑐᓗᐅᖅᖂᓗᐅᖅᓯᒪᕌᖅ.
ᑯᖅᑭᑦᑕᐸᒷᒪᐅᖕᑐᓂ. ᓴᓇᓛᒍᐊᖅᐸᓗᐅᖅᓯᒪᓂᕋᖅ ᖀᕌᓐᖅ ᐅᖅᑯᓄᖀᓂᓗᖂ.
ᓴᓇᔨᒍᒦᕋᓐᓚᑦᑕᐅᖅ ᐊᑭᓪᓐᓄᖃ!

This is my great-grandfather. He is Nana Nora's dad. His name was James Tegeapak.

Nana Nora named me after my great-grandfather.

Everyone tells me I am just like my great-grandfather. He was a great artist. He liked to play guitar. He also liked to make carvings out of wood and soapstone.

I like to build and make stuff with my hands, too!

ᐊᒪᐅᓐᓂᒃ ᐊᑎᖅᑲᖁᒪ, ᑐᖅᓱᕋᖅᑕᐅᕙᒃᑐᖓ ᐱᓐᓇᕆᔭᐅᓪᓗᖓ.

ᓂᖏᐅᕐᒪ ᓄᐊᕋᐅᑉ ᑕᐃᕙᒃᑳᖓ “ᐊᑖᑕ” ᐊᑖᑕᒥᓂᖓᓂᒃ ᐊᑎᖅᑲᖁᒪ.

ᐃᓐᓇᕐᓂᑦ ᐊᑦᑎᐊᕆᔭᐅᔪᖓ “ᑎᒋᐊᐸᒃ,” ᐃᓚᖏᓐᓂᓪᓗ “ᐊᑦᑎᐊᖅ” ᑖᓐᓇ ᑐᑭᓕᒃ “ᐃᓚᓐᓂᒃ.”

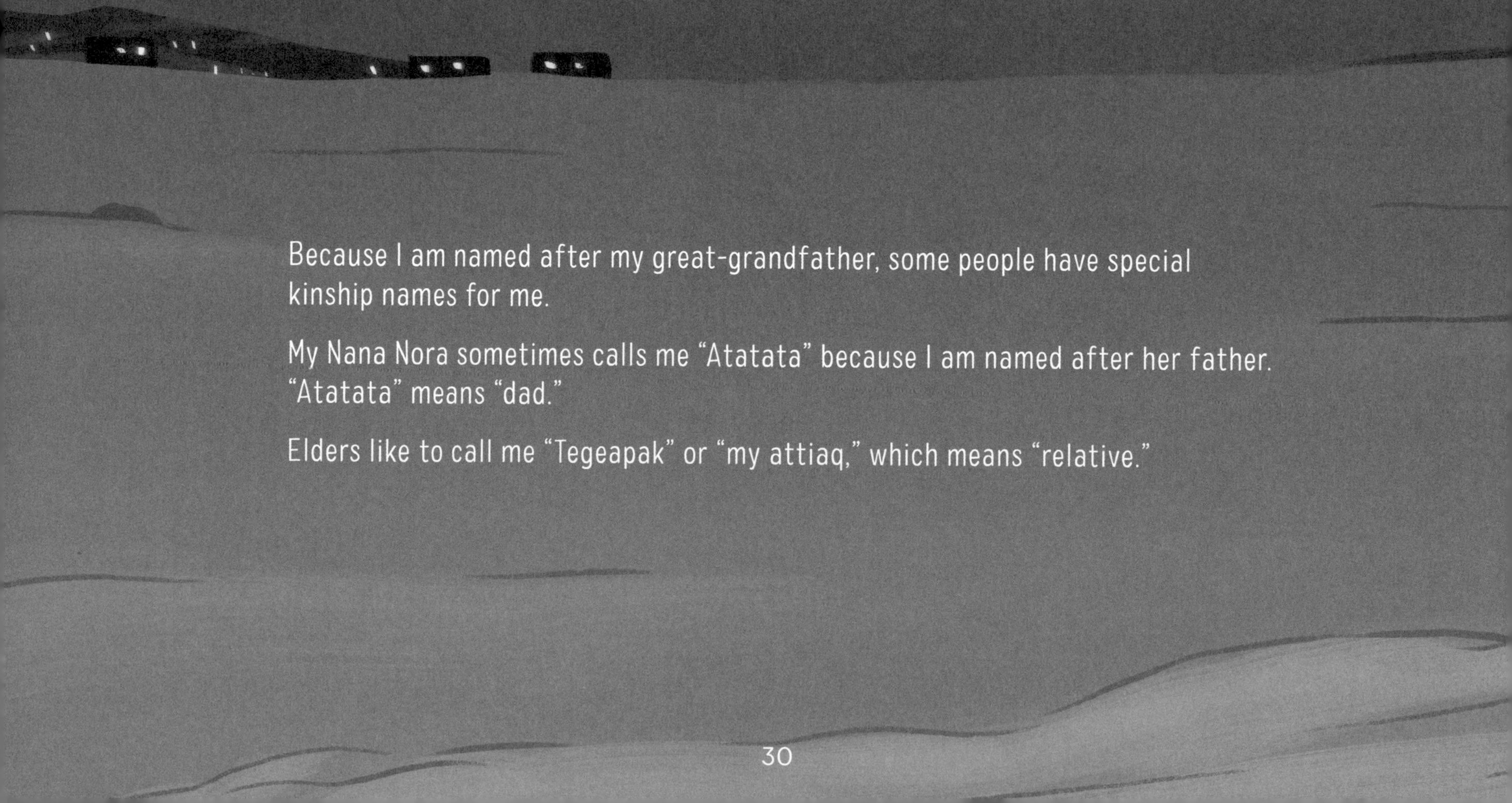

Because I am named after my great-grandfather, some people have special kinship names for me.

My Nana Nora sometimes calls me “Atatata” because I am named after her father. “Atatata” means “dad.”

Elders like to call me “Tegeapak” or “my attiaq,” which means “relative.”

ᑯᑭᒃ, ᓇᐅᓪᓚᖅ, ᐸᓂᒍᓯᖅ, ᑖᒪᓂᒃ ᑎᒋᐊᐸᒃ ᐱᓐᓇᕆᓇᖅᑐᓂᒃ ᐊᑎᖃᓐᓇᑦᑎᐊᖅ!

Kukik, Naullaq, Panigusiq, and Dominic Tegeapak have special names!

ᐅᓂᒃᑳᐅᑎᑎᓪᓗᓂᑎᒍᑦ ᐊᑎᕐᒥᓂᒃ, ᑐᑭᓯᑎᑕᐅᕗᒍᑦ ᐊᑦᑏᓂᐅᑉ ᐱᒻᒪᕆᐅᓂᖓᓂᒃ ᐃᓄᖕᓄᑦ.

By telling us about their names, they are helping us understand why naming is important to Inuit.

ᑭᓇᐅᕕᒃ?

What is your name?